Worship Flow:

28 Ways to Create Great Segues

Jon Nicol

Published by FlingWide Publishing & WorshipTeamCoach.com

First Edition, 2016

Table of Contents

Acknowledgements

Big thanks to Angie Land for the compiling and editing, and Paula Jones for the layout.

Thanks also to my worship teams & pastors at Tiffin Alliance, Reynoldsburg Alliance and Heartland Church for allowing me to try this stuff out.

And huge thanks to my wife Shannon for putting up with my head buried in my Mac as I edited this resource.

Before You Read This...

Worship Flow: 28 Ways to Create Great Segues was originally a series of blog posts on WorshipTeamCoach.com. You can read through this resource front to back, but it's really designed to be more of a reference guide. The chapters are standalone for the most part, but at times will refer back to earlier sections.

One final word before you dive in...

These original blog posts were written in the early days of WorshipTeamCoach.com. As I prepared this resource, reading through my early blog posts was a tad painful. I appreciate Angie Land for doing the hard work to compile, edit and proof these posts. More than once Angie wrote in the notes: "this does not make sense." You're right, Angie, it does not.

So while these posts have been edited, tweaked and edited some more to get rid of the most cringe-worthy moments, there's still a sense of my early writing here. Also, some of the songs and cultural references I updated, some I did not. I hope that's OK for you. To rewrite this material completely would most likely mean this resource would not be released at all.

And, now since this book is about segues, I need a nice transition to the introduction...

Ummm....

I got nothing. Here's the introduction:

Introduction: Transitions Happen

The worship team ends the song.

A smattering of applause from the congregation.

Singers are smiling.

The band looks at the acoustic guitar player.

The acoustic guitar player looks at the keyboard player.

The keyboard player gives him a twitch of the head that says, "You're playing the intro, not me."

The singers continue smiling, but now are glancing over their shoulder to see who's starting the next song.

The guitarist shuffles his charts around and gives the worship leader the universal "Just one moment" sign with his right index finger.

The worship leader wants to give him back a universal sign of his own, but instead says to the congregation, "Let's move into a time of prayer."

That took far longer to read than it did to take place. But if you've ever been a part of a moment like that, especially as a worship leader, it felt like you could have clocked it with a sundial.

Transitions happen. Song to song. Music to preaching. Prayer to offering. They happen. And they can happen just how they happen, or they can happen according to a plan. An unplanned transition is at best a speed bump; at its worst it's a train wreck. When we don't plan a transition, we put a period in where a comma should be. Or a gasp where a gentle inhaled breath should be. Or a fence instead of a gate. Or, well, you get the picture.

The Unplanned Transition: "And Now, Let's Take the Offering..."

An unplanned transition can cause a screeching halt to your service. But more often, the unplanned transition will result in an off-the-cuff attempt at continued forward motion. Frequently it's just a verbal cue from the pastor or worship leader such as, "And at this time, we are going to collect the offering."

Sure, it gets the job done, but I am wondering if there's a better way to move people through the experiences of a worship gathering.

The Unplanned Transition: A Bone

Look at it this way: I've got a great skeleton. It's held me up for over 30 years. It's been broken a half a dozen times or so, but those were pretty much all my fault. Skateboards, jungle gyms, bike meets curb. By sixth grade, the ER staff knew my name. So my skeleton is a good one, but I don't want to see it. If I do see it, other than through an X-ray, something is really wrong. And you can bet that I will be a little preoccupied with that particular bone sticking out of my body.

That's what a poorly planned transition does. It distracts people with an exposed bone (albeit much less gross and icky). It abruptly calls attention to how we are moving to a new element, versus focusing on what the element is. It plucks us out of the moment created by the previous element and plops us into a new one. I don't know about you, but I don't want "plucked" or "plopped" to be action verbs of my worship service (unless it's Jesus doing the plucking and plopping. In that case, just hold on).

So transitions happen, but intentional planning helps us create a seamless movement from experience to experience. I refer to planned transitions as segues. You can still create a bad segue, but the odds for a smoother transition exponentially increase when some thought is put into it.

11

In this resource, we'll be looking at several different segues that cover various elements of the service. This isn't an exhaustive list, but hopefully it will get your wheels turning about different methods to make great transitions in your worship service.

Musical Segues

The First Three Segues

In this first section, we'll look at segues that move us from one song to another within the same key. The first two musical segues simply use the ending of one song to begin the introduction of the next.

Segue #1- Song to Song, Same Key & Tempo

If the tempos are the same, use the ending downbeat of the first song to become the downbeat of the intro for the next song. An example of this is moving from Lincoln Brewster's "Everlasting God" in the key of B (written by Brenton Brown), to Matt Redman's "Blessed Be Your Name" in the same key. The final chorus of "Everlasting God" ends on a B. Simply use that downbeat of the final B chord in "Everlasting God" to begin the U2-esque progression (B > F# > G#m > E) of the "Blessed Be Your Name" intro. By the way, using a single instrument, like the bass or acoustic guitar, to start that intro can create a nice contrast after a big song like "Everlasting God."

This kind of segue—same key, same tempo—is great when you can find it, but don't try to force it. And really, you want a variety of music in your service, so you probably won't get a lot of these.

Segue #2-Song to Song, Same Key; Different Tempo

If the key is the same but the tempo of the second song is slower, try this: simply ritard the last line or tag of the first song to match the tempo of the second song. Another way to transition from a faster to slower song is to reprise a section of the first song at the same tempo as the second song. It's a bit more complicated, but it can move people nicely to a slower song.

An example of this could be moving from "Beautiful One" by Tim Hughes to David Crowder's version of "All Creatures of Our God and King." After ending the song, reprise the chorus one time with lighter instrumentation (and lighter voices), and at a tempo to match the other song. It'll flow like this, *Beautiful One, my soul must sing ... All creatures of our God and King, lift up your voice and with us sing.*

Segue #3-Song to Song, Same Key; Non-Sequential Start

A non-sequential start? OK, it's just a fancy, made-up way to say, "go from the ending of one song to an internal section (like a chorus or bridge) of another song." For example, let's say you're moving from "My Jesus I Love Thee" in E to "Here I Am to Worship" in E. The whole song of "My Jesus I Love Thee" lines up thematically with "Here I Am to Worship", but there's something special about the second verse. Think about moving from the lines...

I love Thee for wearing the thorns on Thy brow / If ever I loved Thee, my Jesus, 'tis now

...into a quiet, maybe even rubato rendering of the bridge of "Here I Am to Worship."

I'll never know how much it costs / to see my sin upon that cross.

Not only does this create a seamless segue from one song to another, but it allows people to experience the lyrics of each song in a new way as they are brought together.

Moving from the end of one song to an internal section of a

song works best when you can match thoughts or concepts from song to song like we just saw. Here are a few other examples of matching the end of one song with an internal section of another:

- "Be Thou My Vision" (traditional hymn) to "You Are My King" (Billy Foote). The final verse of "Be Thou My Vision" is speaking to the High King. Move right from there to the bridge of "You Are My King" (the "You are my King" section). Both can be done in E. To create more dynamics, I do "Be Thou" in Eb for the first 3 verses and modulate to E for the final.

- "Holy, Holy, Holy" (in E, or start in D and play the last verse in E) to the chorus of Chris Tomlin's "We Fall Down."

God, in three Persons, blessed Trinity ... and we cry holy, holy, holy...

An update: Since my church rarely uses "We Fall Down" anymore, I've found moving from the end of Holy, Holy, Holy (key of D) into the chorus of Great I Am (key of D). I tag the last line of the hymn, God in three Persons, blessed Trinity... and instead of ending on a D, I end on a Bm and begin playing and singing the chorus from Great I Am. To make feel right, I just leave out the *hallelujah* and start singing on the *holy, holy* part. Play with that one. It can be really effective.

From that new starting point, determine the best arrangement of the second song. You can also use this segue with songs of different keys, but you will want to make sure you have a smooth modulation to the key of the new song. That's where we'll pick up in the next chapter.

So far we've looked at three different ways to get from one song to the next within the same key. Now we start looking at moving from one key to another.

Segue #4 - Song to Song: The Abrupt Key Change

The abrupt key change, or direct modulation, is simply changing keys without any warning or preparation cadence. A friend of mine always called this the "Barry Manilow key change" when he heard me use it in worship. I took his word for it, since he's the Manilow fan, not me. With no disrespect to "the man who writes the songs that makes the whole world sing", we'll keep referring to this as the "abrupt key change." When it comes to transitioning between songs, you can use this a couple different ways.

First, inside the song. Modulate the first song's last chorus or verse to the key of the next song. This works best if you're going up a whole or half step. Disclaimer: I can't be held responsible for what might happen if you modulate down, or higher than a whole step. I'm not saying it can't work, but...

In the last section, we discussed had an internal key change as a way to prepare for the next songs key. We played the hymn "Holy, Holy, Holy" in the key of D, and then modulated to the key of E for the last verse to prepare for the next song in E. In my stock arrangement for my team, I use a connecting cadence to move to E. In this case, the last note of the melody ends on a "flat 7", or C and then moves down ½ step to variations of the 5 chord of the new key: Bsus, then B/A. (The appendix contains this lead sheet.) However, you don't have to. A whole step is a fairly easy modulation for vocalists to make. You can simply end one verse in D and begin the next one in E.

Let's look at the second way to use the abrupt key change as a way to transition between songs. It's fairly simple: end the first song in its original key, and immediately begin playing the intro to the next song. Easy enough, but there are a few things to consider:

- First, make sure no one in your band is holding out a note from the last song. That will cause widespread cringing and even some bleeding ears.

- Second, the sudden jump in keys could be provocative (in a good way), but make sure it isn't a time during the worship service where you want quiet reflection.

- Third, it can be cool if the whole band modulates at once. But whenever transitioning the band *en masse*, practice it. *A lot.* It only takes one person to change your awesome segue into a "Oh dear Lord what was that?!" moment.

One more thing to consider with this abrupt key change. The key change doesn't always have to go up. Maybe you're ending "How Great is Our God" (key of C), and you decide to go to "Blessed Be Your Name" in B. End "How Great is Our God" with a bar of C and the next bar begins the "Blessed Be Your Name" intro in B. Just be aware that modulating down a key will feel like you're dimming the mood. As long as this is what you're going for, do it.

Whether you go up or down, inside the song or between songs, the abrupt modulation has an unsettling effect. Sometimes you want that, sometimes you don't. But if it works, it's a simple segue to get to where you are going.

In the next chapter we will continue to look musical segues between songs in different keys.

Segue #5 - Using the Five Chord to Transition to Songs in Different Keys

Segue #5...using the five chord? One might think I planned this, but let me assure you: I'm not that bright. However, I am smart enough to know this: music theory freaks a lot of people out. So before we dive in, let be upfront:
We're about to get real with some theory.

I'm going to try to walk the line between over-explaining to accommodate absolute novices, and under-explaining to not bore those who have some theory background. If you're a novice with this stuff, just try these examples on the piano or guitar. The point of the theory is help make sense of and communicate the music in a practical way. So whenever possible, apply these bits of theory to real life music stuff that you already know.

The Five Chord in the traditional numbering system is designated with Roman numeral V. The Nashville number system is gaining massive popularity outside of Tennessee. It designates chords with Arabic numbers. The Five Chord is simply 5 in the Nashville numbering system. I learned music theory originally with the more classically oriented Roman numerals, but have moved to using the Nashville numbers. Throughout the discussion on Five Chords, I will use "5" or "5 chord" when referring to it, unless there are other numbers involved that may confuse things. Then I may use the Roman numeral V or simply spell it out as Five Chord.

So what is the Five Chord? Every key follows the same formula of major and minor chords, which build on each of the intervals in the key. Look at the chart below. You will see that in the key of C, the 5 is G.

Traditional Number	I	ii	Iii	VI	V	vi	vii°
Nashville Number	1	2m	3m	4	5	6m	7dim
Key of C Chords	C	Dm	Em	F	G	Am	Bdim

In terms of segues, the Five Chord of the new key can be used to bridge to the One Chord of the song. Clear as mud? Let me give you an example:

If you're in the key of Eb and the next song is in the key of C, you could simply play a G major chord after the Eb song ends. This will help take the ear from the key of Eb to the key of C.

To create even more aural sympathy[1] for the target key (in this case, C), use the *dominant* 7 version of the 5 chord. The 5 becomes a *dominant* 7 when the b7th interval of the chord is added. In the key of C, the G chord becomes a G7 when the b7th interval above G is added (an F natural). The G7 chord contains the G triad as well as the "flat 7" (a third built diatonically above the 5th).

b7th = f
5th = d
3rd = b
Root=g

The dominant 7 chord is unstable. It feels like it wants to move somewhere. Why? The B and the F in the G7 chord create a tritone[2]. A tritone is an augmented 4th or a flat 5th interval. Play the B just below middle C on your piano and the F just above it.

Icky, huh?

It becomes a lot more tolerable with the root and 5th added, but it still naturally wants to resolve:

---

1 OK, I might've just made this term up. In fact, I just googled "aural sympathy" and got nothing. But hey, it sounded pretty impressive, didn't it? What I'm saying here is simply, "Prepare people's ears for the new key."

2 Guitarists, to hear a tritone (or b5 interval), play your open B string and the F on your high E string (1st string, 1st fret). The sound it makes is uglier than your sophomore homecoming date. Oh, you married your sophomore homecoming date? Ummm...yeah...so how abut that tritone?

G7			C
b7th	f	Wants to resolve a 1/2 step down.	e (3rd)
5th	d	No real tension. Can go down to the c or up to the e.	c (Root) e (3rd)
3rd	b	Wants to resolve 1/2 step up.	c (Root)
Root	g	Common tone.	g (5th)

In this G7 chord, the B and the F together create the unstable tritone. Our ears crave a resolution to the dissonance of that chord.

If all this is about is as understandable as quantum physics, take heart. It's all learnable, and believe it or not, it is (sometimes) actually useful. Let me get really practical. In order to use this transition, all you need to know is the Five Chord of the key you will be going to. Take a look at this chart:

Five Chord		Target Key
G7	»	C
D7	»	G
A7	»	D
E7	»	A
B7	»	E
F#7	»	B
C#7	»	F#
Db7	»	Gb
Ab7	»	Db
Eb7	»	Ab
Bb7	»	Eb
F7	»	Bb
C7	»	F

If you are in the key of G and moving to A, the Five Chord of A is E. Playing E as a transition chord will help move the listener's ear to the key of A. For example, we're doing "10,000 Reasons" (Matt Redman) in the key of G and moving to "God is Able" (Hillsong) in the key of A:

The first song will end with *sing like never before, O my soul, I'll worship Your holy Name*, and move into the outro, which ends on a G chord. Let the final chord ring out for a few beats, then play an E or E7 for a measure and move into the verse or intro of "God is Able."

There are a number of variations of the Five Chord transition. Here are some more common ones:

5sus4 (R, 4th, 5th) Example: Gsus4 (G, C, D)

This is often just called the "sus chord." The 4 is implied. So you'll see Gsus4 often written as Gsus.

A related variation of the sus4 is the "add4."[3] While we don't have time to explain all nuances and differences between sus4 and add4, the bottom line is this: Suspend means "replace the 3rd" and add means "add to the third". So with a suspended 4th chord, the 4th interval replaces the 3rd.

This sus4 chord helps draws the listener's ear to the new key because of the sus4 note is actually the root of the new

---

3 The "add11"chord is related to this. The 11th interval is simply octave above the 4th. In very simplistic terms, it implies that, besides the 4th being added, the 7th of the chord is also present. Music theorists will argue a certain order of these notes. I don't really care since I'm a guitarist and can't physically play them in that order anyway.

key. So in the example above, moving from G to A, the Five Chord of A is E. If we make that an Esus4, guess what the sus4 note in that chord is: A.

Another way to use the sus4 is to help soften the dominant 7 chord. 5^7 is often a little too bright, so the sus4 can be added to that as well.

5^7sus^4 (R, 4th, 5th, B7th) Example: G^7sus^4 (G, C, D, F)

Play a G7. Now play a G7sus4. Notice that it doesn't seem to have the dissonance of the G7? That's because by replacing the B note with a C, we removed the tritone – that $^b5$ interval between the B and the F. But it does still want to resolve back to the C.

You will often see this chord written as a hybrid slash chord: 4/5. An example of this is C/D. It's a C triad (C,E,G) with a D in the bass. The notes spell out a D9sus chord, which is the same as a D7sus with an added E (the 9th of D). Another variation of this hybrid chord that creates a V9sus is the 2m7/5, e.g. Am7/D. This now simply contains the 5th of the V7sus. Using hybrid chords like this allows the arranger to spell out more exactly how the chord is to be played.

The 5^{7SUS} to 5^7 Progression

Another option is to use a combination: resolve 5^{7sus4} to the 5^7 before moving to the root chord of the new key. Or, re-solve 5sus to 5, then to the root. This progression creates movement within the chord: the sus4 resolves down a half step to the 3rd, which also then moves back up a half step to the root of the new key. Try this progression moving from the key of D to the key of E:

This resolve from the 5^{sus7} to the 5^7 is a way to move people along more smoothly.

In the next chapter, we'll add a few more tricks to our Five Chord, creating an even greater sense of movement as you segue from a one song to another in a different key.

Segue #6: The "4 to 5" and "2m7 to 5" Progressions

For this next segue, we're going to continue using the Five Chord. But now we'll be adding some common transition chords with it.

The 4 to 5 Progression

The 4 to 5 progression is as common in worship music as corn dogs at a county fair. In the key of C, the 4 and 5 chords are F and G, respectively. Instead of going right for the 5^7 transition, you can move the listener's ear along by entering the new key with the 4 chord.

In the last segue, we looked at moving from the key of D to the key of E by way of the B or B7 chord, which is the 5 chord of the key of E. Let's now add the 4 chord to the transition.

The A chord is part of the key D, so moving to it in this transition didn't sound like a change until the B was played. The A chord (4 of the new key) helps soften that transition.

Let's look at a transition in which the first key and the second key do not share common chords.

In this case, the A is a much brighter departure from the key of C. And you don't just have to settle for the simple A to B (4 to 5), but look at coloring the 5 chord with the dominant 7, sus4, 7sus4, and so on, in order to create even more movement and pull from one key to the next.

The 2m to 5 Progression

Another variation of "4 to 5" progression is the "2m to 5." This is a staple progression in jazz, but it's also commonly used in worship music. Instead of utilizing the 4 chord to move to the 5 chord, go to the two minor (2m) chord first. Play through this transition from the key of C to the key of A utilizing the 2m chord.

The 2m chord is closely related to 4, which is why this transition sounds similar to the 4 to 5 progression. But the 2m creates a different color and mood than the 4. In the progression above, you will notice that by using the 2m7 (Bm7), we found a chord that was only a half step away from the 1 chord (C) of the original key. This example sets us up for the next segue, which looks for a natural sounding chord "trail" from one key to the next.

Segue #7 - Finding a Chord Trail to the New Key

The gist of this segue is finding a "path" of chords that lead to the new key. Here's an example:

Key of C to Key of D♭ (half step up)

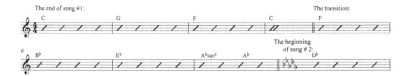

Moving back to the F chord created a smoother transition to the Bb chord (because they share two common keys), which allowed a smooth transition to the Eb. This created a similar bridge to the final chord of the transition, which is the 5^{7sus} (A^{bsus}) of the new key: Db.

That example used chords that were a 4th and 5th apart. The C in the fourth measure became the 5 chord of the key of F. Then the F chord became the 5 chord of the key of Bb. Then the Bb became the 5 chord of the Eb. Then the Eb became the 5 chord of the Ab. And that became the 5 chord of the new key: Db. And you just became light-headed. Sorry, that was a lot to take in.

Here's an example of a more linear path to the same place.

C to Db (Half step up)

This transition still used chords that were a 3rd or 6th apart, or a 4th or 5th apart, but the use of inversions (a non-root chord tone in the bass of the chord, known also as "slash" chords) gave the feel of a step motion since the bass line was walking down a half step each time.

Now, you will probably only want to use an elaborate key change like these in certain parts of your service. This kind of transition is perfect for underscoring a prayer: the team ends one song in C and the next is in Db. The pastor decides to pray at that point and the pianist (or the guitarist, if he's brave and has a capo) can meander over these chords during the prayer. If the transition is played slowly, lingering on each chord, the congregation won't even know they've been taken to a new key.

There are countless ways to do this Chord Trail transition. Here are just a few more examples:

C to D (whole step up)

This one is much shorter. It utilized a "flat seven" chord (^{b}7), in this case Bb, to bridge to the Asus, the 5 of D. The ^{b}7 chord really grabs the ear and takes us immediately out of the key. In the bonus section, you see how to utilize the ^{b}7 in the arrangement of "Holy, Holy, Holy."

You can also use minor chords along with inversions to help move you to the next key:

C to D (whole step up)

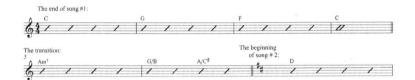

Again, there are a bazillion ways to move from any key to any other key. Just play around with chord trails when you are working on your song to song transitions.

A word of warning: I like chord trail transitions, but I have learned simpler is usually better. For instance, I've come up with some really sweet modulations that sound awesome.

On just my guitar.

In my office.

Alone.

With the door closed.

But reality has a way of poking holes in our ideal arrangements. I welcome it as a learning experience when I find out at rehearsal that one of my "awesome transitions" isn't so awesome. But I don't love the learning experience that happens in front of a large audience when I find out on Sunday.

So, yeah, keep it simple.

Segue #8 - The Lingering Four Chord

Sometimes during worship you want to move from one element to the next quickly. Other times, you just want to stay in the moment, in that place where people are connecting with God. Hopefully you have had those moments when it would just feel wrong to put the end cap on the song by playing the final chord of the song. A great place to go instead is the Four Chord (IV or 4).

The Four Chord is simply that: the chord built on the 4th interval of the key. F is the 4 chord of the key of C:

1	2m	3m	4
C	Dm	Em	F

As much as the 5 chord (especially 5^7) wants to move back to the root, the 4 chord doesn't seem to have that much desire to go anywhere.

Let's look at Tim Hughes song "Here I Am to Worship" (in the key of E). This song is a classic example of the "Lingering Four Chord." The last chord of the last lines of both the chorus and the bridge is A (or A2). By landing on that very stable, but very *not final* chord, Hughes was able to build in what worshipers want: a moment just to be, to linger in the presence of God.

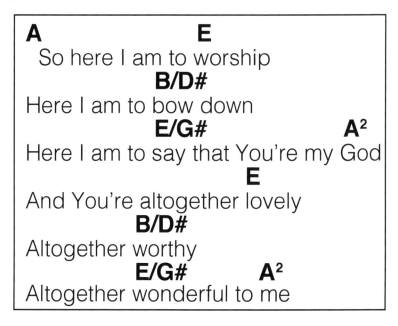

We can just hang at the end of those lines, stop the rhythm, let the guitar or piano lightly play that A2 and just be in the moment. No one needs lead sheets or video screens at that moment.

What about songs that don't have that built-in linger factor? Most of the time, a song can end with the 4 chord instead of the 1 chord.

Here is "Crown Him with Many Crowns" ending on the 1:

It feels absolutely done.

Now play and sing it ending on the 4:

It feels like there's a place to hang out now, doesn't it?

After you've hung out, you can:

1. end on the 1 chord
2. simply let the 4 chord fade away, or
3. use the 4 chord as the beginning of a transition to another song.

Review some of the transitions we've already talked about. You'll begin to see ways that you can marry a lot of these segues together.

Bonus Musical Segue – The Pad

When I originally wrote this series, I didn't use this particular segue. But now I use it all the time. What changed? For the longest time, I had a team that contained pianists, not keyboard players. You know the difference:

- The pianist plays the piano. And even if it's a synth or digital piano, the only setting they can find is the Steinway patch.
- The keyboard player uses the keyboard to not only play the piano, when needed, but also to make a variety of sonic contributions.

One huge contribution keyboard players make is "the pad." *Pad* can mean a lot of different things in music. In the styles of rock and pop that mostly influence our worship music, a pad is a sustaining sound that has little or no rhythm. It often created by a synth sound, some strings, an organ or any combination of. It's subtle and glues together all the instruments.

One of easiest ways to create a smooth segue from song to song is simply fade in a pad in the key of the new song. If the songs are in the same key, even easier. Let the pad hang on through the gap. Presto! No dead air.

Another option is using a product called Pad Loops made by Shalon Palmer (padloops.com). These are pad sounds in every key and can be played from an iPod or other mp3 player along during your worship songs. At the time of this writing, a set of pads for every key only run $30. That's cheaper than buying a new keyboard.

Non-Musical Segues

Over the last few chapters, we were looking primarily at musical transitions. These next six non-musical segues are designed to go from song to song, into a song from a non-musical element, or out of a song to non-musical element.

Segue #9: The Clap Offering

One of my drummers at my last church asked me why I always planned musical segues between songs. He had attended a large Vineyard church and commented how they would just end a song and count off to the next. Having been to that church, I knew that after most of the faster or bigger songs the congregation spontaneously applauds and cheers. That clap offering *is* the segue.

Applause is a natural occurrence in some churches; in other churches, it would precipitate the forced resignation of the worship pastor and the revocation of several memberships.

If you are somewhere in the middle where clapping is okay, but just not natural, here are steps to cultivate spontaneous, post-song clapping in worship.

- Teach that clapping is biblical and that the applause isn't for the people on stage. This doesn't need its own sermon; it can be done in 90 seconds during a call to worship. Say something like this:

   Psalm 47[4] says this:

---

4 Psalm 47:1-2 (NLT)

Come, everyone! Clap your hands!
Shout to God with joyful praise!
For the Lord Most High is awesome.
He is the great King of all the earth.

During our time of worshiping through music this morning, one of the ways we can worship God is by applauding for Him. We're not clapping for music, the musicians, or how great we just sang as a congregation. We are simply celebrating the Great King who has invited us into His presence.

- Prompt the congregation. During that same service, after a song where clapping would feel appropriate ("Softly and Tenderly" is probably *not* one of those songs), say to the congregation,

  "Let's applaud for the Lord."

  You as the leader will set the tone for this. Look up as you clap. God isn't exclusively "in the sky," but our gazing upwards is symbolic of His otherness, His transcendence and His kingly majesty.

- Prepare your band members before the service to applaud at specific moments. Make sure they aren't taking a posture of "receiving" applause. That will sour the applause for a lot of people. Having your band participate does two things:

1. It says to the congregation that this is NOT about us. It takes the focus off the music and band and puts it on the King.

2. It gives people permission to clap. By seeing the team applaud, people will feel more comfortable to do so.

- Repeat this encouragement at least once a service for a couple months. It will take a while for it to become a natural part of your worship gathering experience. But if you keep encouraging and modeling it, applause will begin to happen.

- Another way to encourage clap offerings is to "plant" clappers in the congregation. That sounds a little underhanded, but hang with me for a moment. At a previous church I served in, we were *not* a clapping church, unless someone mentioned the Ohio State Buckeyes. (That was probably part of the issue: scarlet and gray idolatry.) There were a few people in my church that I knew wanted to clap, but didn't want to offend. I encouraged them to clap and affirmed that it was a good thing. Two or three pairs of hands clapping are often all that's needed to start a full applause.

Clapping, like any element in your worship service, can become an empty ritual if it loses its heart motivation. Don't just use clapping as a way to get from one song to the next. But if it is a way that your congregation worships, or has the potential to, by all means use it. The clap offering can be a very viable segue.

So one question remains: How do you use the clap offering?

Realistically, an applause moment will take only about five to seven seconds. But in that time, the drummer can be counting off the next song, capos can be taken off/put on, and music pages can be turned. If the same things happened with no clapping or other segue element, it could feel awkward. So don't discount what a five second buffer can give your team when it comes to transitions.

Segue #10: The Count-In

Uno, dos, tres, cuatro!, or the English version, is sometimes all the segue you need from one song to the next.

This is especially effective when you have cultivated the last segue (the clap offering). As the applause is dying down, the drummer can click off a four count with his sticks or on his high hat. Even if there is no clapping, that simple count-in will be enough to give the feeling of transition from one song to another. When it comes to the count-in, here are some things to think about:

Who's counting in?

In a perfect world, the drummer is. In that same perfect world, he's marked the beats-per-minute (BPM) for each song and might even have a metronome handy to make sure he's got the tempo down. At a previous church I served at, I could throw out a random BPM to one of my drummers, and he'd click it off faster than I could enter it in to my metronome. He was always spot on, and a little freakish.

If you think your drummer may not be the best to count your band in, give that duty to your lead musician or music director, the person that the rest of the team looks to. That's probably you. So don't be afraid to count out loud with some confidence.

Does every song need a count-in? No. Here's a good rule of thumb for count-ins: if the whole band is starting at once, you NEED a solid count-in. For songs starting with only one instrument, likely a guitar or piano, a count-in usually isn't needed. (Exception: if your player doesn't have the tempo internalized, then letting him start the song could likely be the precursor to a slow train wreck or a fast plunge off a cliff. In that case, count him in.)

Is it always 1,2,3,4? Not necessarily. If you are in $^3/_4$ time, you certainly don't want to count-off in $^4/_4$ time. Even if you are in 4, you often don't need all four beats. Counting two beats (3,4) is often adequate to communicate the tempo. This is especially effective when only two instruments are starting together, like the acoustic guitarist and the drummer.

How soon should the count-in start? If there will be no applause or any other segue element, you probably need to start the count-in before the last song dies out. Allow the last note or beat of the song to ring. As the rest of the band is holding out their last note, the drummer can begin to count in the new song. It will feel like a seamless transition.

Among all the different segues we have looked at, this is probably one of the simplest. Just remember, there are three kinds of people in this world: those who can count, and those who can't. (Did you catch that? It was joke...*three* kinds of people...*never mind*.)

[An Update]

Since writing this original blog post, I've transitioned my team to using in-ear monitors and a click track. Some say that squashes the flow, or creativity, or even the Holy Spirit. But they have the right to make spiritualized excuses as to why their band doesn't play in time together.

OK, that was a tad harsh. Sorry.

Contrary to the naysayers, I've found the constraints of the click track to be freeing. But the click does add an extra element do deal with during this transition. Fortunately, my drummers are on it and can start and stop the click between crashes and kicks. It's like they have a third arm.

Segue #11: The Prayer

Okay, time for true confessions: in the not too distant past, I told my team's vocal leader for that week to throw in a prayer between two songs. Our sparse band that week didn't allow for another musician to handle the introduction, and I had a capo and a patch change that would've created too much dead space. I try to plan for things like this, but I missed it.

Let me get this out there first: corporate prayer isn't a segue. It's a crucial part of our worship experience. Time should be allotted for it. Planning should be put into both *what* is prayed and *how* it's prayed. And we should be open for left turns that the Holy Spirit prompts for our public prayers. But as we plan the rhythm and flow of our worship gatherings, prayer can effectively bridge two songs.

When it comes to using prayer as a bridge (and not abusing it as a space filler), here are a few prayer personalities to avoid.

The Over Pray-er. This can either be in frequency or length. For some it's easy to pray before, after, and during songs. And for some over pray-ers, getting them to pray a brief prayer is like getting the *aurora borealis* to shine in Texas.

The Intimate Pray-er. This is the person who closes his eyes and all others disappear, just him and God. Not a bad place to be as a worshiper, but as a leader, and especially leading public prayer, the congregation is going to feel a little left out.

The Lyric Pray-er. "Lord, we lift your name on high, Lord, we love to sing your praises, we're so glad you're in our lives, we're so glad you came to save us." The words are great. The truth is there. But most of the time, reiterating several lines of song lyrics just sounds contrived.

I think the key to bridging songs with prayer is *intentionality*. We need to think through what song preceded the prayer and what song or songs are coming. We should ask ourselves:

- *What kind of prayer should be prayed here?* Adoration? Supplication? Confession? A brief prayer between songs shouldn't try to cover all the bases, but focus on one aspect of approaching God.
- *What will draw the congregation in and allow them to participate in this prayer?*

Honestly, I think the way pastors and other leaders lead out in prayer is one of the most disengaging acts during corporate worship (Oh wait, I forgot about the announcements. OK, second most disengaging act). If our congregations are full of experienced prayer warriors who have learned to engage and agree while someone else is praying, then we're okay. But most people, I would guess, check out sometime between, "O Gracious Heavenly Father" and "in Jesus' Name, Amen". Maybe it's spiritual immaturity. Maybe it's cultural ADD. Maybe it's just me.

As much as we try to engage people in singing, what if we tried to engage them in prayer, even for a brief moment between songs? This topic deserves a whole chapter (and probably a book) to flesh out. But it's something for us to think about as we insert prayer into our services.

Lastly, when it comes to using prayer as a bridge between songs, consider lightly underscoring it with a piano or keyboard, or a guitar. Some call it a musical bed. Others call it noodling. Whatever you call it, it helps carry people from the song through the prayer and into the next song. You may want to revisit some of the earlier chapters that discussed musical segues between songs for ideas on what to play during the prayer.

Segue #12: Scripture

Part I

Transitioning from one song to another with scripture is like a segue on steroids (without the rage). Here are several reasons why.

It's a Compass

Using scripture, especially amongst man-made songs, serves as a *compass*. Are the songs we choose grounded in the Bible? We sure try. Are many of them inspired? Yes, but "little-i" inspired, not *Inspired*—as in God-breathed, inerrant Word of God, needle-pointing True North inspired. As we flow from one song to another, a segue through scripture re-centers our heart and reorients our minds.

It's Common Ground

As I lead my congregation from the hymn "Holy, Holy, Holy" into "Revelation Song" via a reading from Revelation 5, I'm creating common ground for a diverse crowd. For instance, the older generation in my church has a long history with "Holy, Holy, Holy." This can't be said of many in the younger generations. Likewise, "Revelation Song" may move many of the Xers, Millennials, and (thanks to Phillips, Craig and Dean) the Boomers, but our Builders may not connect as well. To bring in chapter 5 of John's Revelation, it reflects where we've been ("Holy, Holy, Holy") and where we're going ("Revelation Song"), and is neither old or new. It is ancient and future. The living and active Word becomes a common ground for the generations.

It Provides a Unique Context

We don't know what God might be doing in people as they encounter a scripture in a different context. Maybe someone slogged through Job a few years ago during a painful *One Year through the Bible* attempt. Imagine him now seeing chapter 9 as your team moves out of "Indescribable" into another song describing His greatness. His ears are still ringing with *"you place the stars in the sky and you call them by name,"* and then he encounters:

4 *His wisdom is profound, his power is vast.*
      Who has resisted him and come out unscathed?
5 *He moves mountains without their knowing it*
      and overturns them in his anger.
6 *He shakes the earth from its place*
      and makes its pillars tremble.
7 *He speaks to the sun and it does not shine;*
      he seals off the light of the stars.
8 *He alone stretches out the heavens*
      and treads on the waves of the sea.
9 *He is the Maker of the Bear and Orion,*

the Pleiades and the constellations of the south.
[10] He performs wonders that cannot be fathomed,
*   miracles that cannot be counted.*   (Job 9 NIV)

It's a Catalyst

Our well-meant words of encouragement and cajoling from the stage hold nothing compared to the Word.

> *For the word of God is living and active. Sharper than any double-edged sword, it penetrates even to dividing soul and spirit, joints and marrow; it judges the thoughts and attitudes of the heart.* Hebrews 4:12

Scripture, through the illumination of the Holy Spirit, can stir and convict, rip and tear, melt and move. It puts the responsibility for changing hearts squarely back into the lap of Jesus Christ, where it belongs. It's not our job. That, friends, is very good news.

Segue #12: Scripture

Part II

We talked in the last section about why scripture is a segue on steroids. Now let's look at *how* we can use this strongman segue to carry us between songs.

A Connector of Themes

As I write this, this Sunday we're singing "Crown Him with Many Crowns" and then moving into Hillsong's "Hosanna." The "Hosanna" lyrics are heavily drawn from Psalm 24. As the last chord of "Crown Him" is ringing out, the leader will read verses 24:7-10, which connects to the King theme in this song. The leader will conclude with these verses.

> *Who is he, this King of glory?*
> *The LORD Almighty*
> *he is the King of glory.*

From there the vocalists will begin singing the opening lines of "Hosanna": *I see the King of Glory.*

This scripture connects the different but related themes between these two songs. It also helps transition us from the big ending of a big anthem, to the more subdued beginning of "Hosanna." And here's a bonus: we're revisiting Psalm 24 during the instrumental of "Hosanna" by using verses 3-6, which is a great set up for the bridge.

Stories

Often we look for verses from Psalms or an epistle, but don't forget about narrative passages of scripture. Once I wanted to use John 11:25-26 (where Jesus tells Martha that he is resurrection and the life) to segue into a song focused on new life. Some wild hair struck and I decided to use the whole passage, starting at verse 17 and concluding with Martha's confession of belief and faith in Jesus as the Messiah. I honestly don't remember what specific songs I was bridging that Sunday, but the power of reading Jesus' (and Martha's) words in context of the story is something I won't forget. As I read Christ's words, "I am the resurrection..." a flood of emotion hit me. I could barely finish. Not only did the story help deepen the experience of verses 25-26, but that scripture then stayed with us as we sang about new life in Christ.

Montage

Don't limit yourself to one passage. Maybe you are singing the Neale/Nordoff tune "Your Great Name" and moving to Baloche's "Your Name." Try a montage of scriptures that focus on the Name of God. The bonus section contains an example of this as well as other "swipe copies" of scripture montages I've created.

Multiple Voices

When using longer passages or multiple scriptures (like the montages), consider using more than one reader. Multiple readers can add energy and variety. This could be a whole chapter in itself, but I'll move on with one admonishment: encourage your readers to use inflection and emotion and at a pace that doesn't drag.

A Great Planning Tool to Help

Outside of personal quiet time, I use BibleGateway.com more than I use a hard copy Bible. Within a couple clicks you can see scores of translations for the passage you are looking up. Can't remember the reference? Just type in the phrase or word you're looking for. The keyword search also made it easy to assemble the scripture montages. As you are planning these segues, having a tool like this gold.

Underscoring

Should we put music under these scripture readings? When it's a short scripture connecting two songs with dis-parate styles or keys, don't use music. Let the reading do the heavy lifting of the segue. Also, the non-musical mo-ment will cleanse our sonic palette for the next song.

However, during longer scripture readings, I always try to use a musical bed, or an underscore. You can allow the reader to fly solo for a few moments after the previous song ends, but ease in some guitar or piano noodling that can easily take the team to the intro of the next song.

We'll also talk a little more about using scripture as a segue when we look at connecting non-musical elements of the service.

Segue #13 - *Selah*

Selah is one of those words that Biblical scholars have to guess at. Some think it's a musical notation. Others believe it's a directive to stop the reading or singing. I like how the Amplified Bible describes *Selah*: "pause, and think of that."

Our cultural ADD doesn't allow us to "pause and ponder" well. We pause, but it's usually to turn our attention to something else. Stopping to be quiet? That's tough. But it could be one of the most neglected, but needed practices in our churches. And just like prayer and scripture, the purposeful pause of *Selah* can be both a segue and its own element of worship.

One of my favorite instance of a *Selah* in the book of Psalms is in chapter 77. Asaph is in a bad way. God does not seem to be there. Verse after verse he focuses on his present anguish and God's inactivity. Then we have our first *Selah*.[5] He's now digging through his memories of the good days when God was there and songs poured from his heart. This only makes the present pit worse. It takes Asaph to where his heart has rarely gone, asking, "has God forgotten me?"

And now we have my favorite *Selah*. After sinking deep in-

---

5 You won't see the Selah markings in the latest version of the NIV. If you want to see them, try the ESV. The NLT translates it as "interlude."

side himself, Asaph pauses and begins to look outside of both himself and his past experiences. He begins to think about God, His mighty works, His awesome wonder. At the apex of Asaph's gut-wrenching song he declares:

Your ways, O God, are holy.
What god is so great as our God

Asaph's heart had turned inward on itself. God couldn't be found there. But he turned and acknowledged through the pain that not only is God holy, but His *ways* are holy. Asaph doesn't understand it. His pain isn't gone. His circumstances haven't changed, but his focus has.

And that might be the power of a *Selah*; a pause to allow us to wrestle with our circumstances, our pain, our shame, our sin and idolatry, and see that God is there. Not inside our self-focused heart, but outside. Outside waiting to come in and be our focus, our center. And it's out of a *Selah* like that we sing not the *"I, me and we"* songs, but a song that proclaims…

Your ways, O God, are holy.
What god is so great as our God

Segue #14: A Talking Transition

Words are very
unnecessary
they can only do harm
("Enjoy the Silence" by Depeche Mode)

From segues #13 to #14, we swing from silence as a segue to a talking transition. Honestly, after my bumbling beginnings as a young worship leader, I took the Depeche Mode lyrics to heart. Better to let my guitar or a scripture carry us from one song to the next.

Some people have the opposite approach. The worst is when you have a worship leader who wants to be a preacher. He's exegeting Isaiah 6 between a Chris Tomlin tune and a Hillsong chorus, while the bass player's nodding off from 10 minutes of inactivity. Senior pastors will back me up on this one: *we need the "less is more" approach when it comes to talking.*

I need to confess something, however. I tended to think my golden silence was some sort of holy high road that was much preferable to over-talking. While it might've been more welcome than a three-point sermon following the opening song, it was just an avoidance of the preparation it takes to make a great verbal segue.

And that's the key to great verbal segues—preparation: Think it through. Pray it through. Let it simmer.

- Read the lyrics of the song you're leaving. Ask, "Where have we just been?"
- Read the lyrics of the song you're moving to. Ask, "What is the moment we're moving towards?"

Direction

As you craft your verbal segue, pray for clarity of direction. We have a Point A and a Point B. What should I say to get us there? (Remember the straight-line principle.)

Think of your verbal segue as a mini journey. Every journey has a beginning, middle and end. The *beginning* needs to move us out of the first song. The *end* moves us into the second song. The *middle* is the meat. The *meat* can tie the two songs together, but it doesn't have to. It can prepare us for the "worship moment" contained in the next song.

Let's say we're going from Tomlin's "Our God" to "Revelation Song" this Sunday. I might plan to say something like this as "Our God" ends:

"Our God IS greater. No matter what we can imagine or think about God, He's always greater. Whatever we think about His love and grace, His love and grace are always greater than we can imagine. God is always greater. And even when we see His glory with our own eyes, we will never exhaust the praises and honor that can be given to Him. John describes in Revelation 4 that those gathered around the throne never stop worshiping Him day and night. Let's worship Him and His greatness with the words that are being sung even now around His throne."

A so-so segue. Given a little more thought, this verbal segue could be improved. But it's a start. As you're preparing and thinking through your transition, consider a few things:

Be Brief

One of my favorite movies is the Clooney/Pitt remake of *Ocean's 11*. Pitt's character, Rusty, is giving instructions to Linus (played by Matt Damon) about how to pass as a Nevada state gaming official. One of his pieces of advice: "Don't use seven words when four will do."

Brevity for brevity's sake isn't the point. The point is to be *succinct*. Merriam-Webster defines *succinct*, well, succinctly: *"marked by compact precise expression without wasted words."* Most of us don't have the gift of being succinct on the fly. It takes a little preparation.

Besides the Five Bs *(Be brief, baby, be brief)*, here are some other Be's.

Be Specific

"God is great and we should praise him forever" is a true and good statement. But a few specifics will give the congregation something of substance to connect with. Using Revelation 4, even paraphrased as it was, gave us an event to relate to: the past, present and future worship around the throne of God.

Be Memorable

This goes against another piece of Rusty's advice to Linus. But we're trying to facilitate worship, not outwit a mark. If we're going to say something, let's say something worth remembering. People aren't going to remember your whole segue. But try to make some part of the main point, or the meat, easy to remember. Memorability is succinctness coupled with repetition. Check out the repetition In the example above:

> 1st sentence: "greater"
> 2nd sentence: "He's always greater."

3rd sentence: "His love and grace are always greater"
4th sentence: "God is always greater."

The fourth sentence is, hopefully, the memorable takeaway. As people's voices are pouring out the high praise of "Revelation Song," their hearts are bursting with the thought "God is even greater than this!"

Be Accurate

In the last segue, I talked about the Selah in Psalm 77. When I originally wrote this post, I attributed the Psalm to David. It wasn't one of David's. Asaph wrote it. Authorship didn't change the point I made. But an inaccuracy can discredit the veracity of the main point.

Let's be real: worship leaders are often frequent offenders of using unchecked paraphrases of scripture. This is a real issue. If I make an inaccurate statement in worship, it has two ill effects. One, those who catch the mistake are immediately taken out of the flow of worship because their BS alarm just went off. Two, those who don't catch it might believe it and repeat it, especially if I've done a good job of saying something memorable. So take a minute to check your facts and references.

Be Careful

Avoid controversial issues. I'm not talking about what people in the world or liberal churches would call controversial: the virgin birth, the deity of Christ, the resurrection, etc. We can be bold about what we believe. I'm talking about the gray area stuff. It's the stuff that no matter which side you fall on, it probably won't keep you out of heaven. A worship service segue is probably not the time to bring up the role of women in the church, for instance, or spark a Calvinism-Arminian debate.

Be Submissive

If you're new or haven't yet gained the confidence of your senior pastor, worship pastor, or elder you are serving under, submit your segues in writing to him or her before Sunday. He may not ask you to do this, but it can be good to create trust and solicit advice for improvement. At some point, if he's not a control freak, he'll probably say, "I trust you," and give you free reign in this area.

Be Confident

A lot of us musicians are great behind the guitar or piano. But the microphone becomes a scary place when you take away our music. Confidence comes from preparation—not just for what you're going to say, but how you're going to say it. Practice it, just like you would a song.

Be Conversational

The danger of writing something out is that it could sound too formal. Remember, you're talking to friends. This is especially important if you're telling a personal story. If it sounds like something you wrote out as an assignment for a class, it won't ring authentic. So as you prepare and practice, work at keeping it natural and "you."

Be Spontaneous(?!)

I know. That goes against everything I just laid out. But the more we plan and practice our segues, the easier it will be to go off-the-cuff when we feel the prompting of the Holy Spirit.

When it comes to verbal segues, is there a rule for how long and how often they should be done? It's really up to you and what you think connects with your church. I personally would not plan more than one verbal segue per service. In many services, I don't have any spoken transitions between songs. I still have the tendency to err on the side of keeping my mouth shut more often than not, at least during the worship service. If I could learn that in other areas, my life might be a lot simpler.

Segue #15: The Offering

Part I

"We'll be taking the offering in a few moments." (Hint to ushers: please come to the front)

Some off-the-cuff announcements, then, "And now, as the ushers come forward, we'll be receiving our tithes and offering." (Hint to ushers, *please* come to the front.)

Pause. The pastor looks back to see the one usher give the sideways head jerk to two other ushers still in their seats.

"Alright, AS THE USHERS COME FORWARD, let's prayer for our tithes and offerings." (A slightly stronger hint.)

Pause, as the ushers come forward.

They've arrived. The pastor's chest starts to untighten just a little. "Let's pray."

When it comes to a transition in worship, each additional person that is involved increases the chance for derailment. *Exponentially*. The segue to the offering is one of those transitions. Here are all the potential people involved:

- The music/worship leader ending the song.

- The pastor or elder stepping up to pray for the offering.
- The worship tech turning on the pulpit mic or pastor's wireless mic.
- The ushers.
- Whatever element you're using to fill the time as the plates are passed.

If you have video, then you have worship techs to depend on. For a musical element, you'll have to factor in the soloists, band, and/or accompaniment tracks.

With all those moving parts, it's no wonder that for so many churches this is the segment that grinds momentum to a halt. Here are some ideas to create smoother movement in and out of the offering.

Script out your services

The offering is something that most pastors have done for so long, they don't think that a script is needed. But any segue in or out of a service element, especially as one that involves as many people as the offering does, needs to be planned carefully. A few thoughts about scripts:

- The act of writing it out is at least 75% of the work. It forces you to think through all the details.

- Get other eyes on it before finalizing it. Ever forgotten to put in the dismissal for kids church? Your kids' ministry leader or a mother of preschoolers would have caught it.
- Put it in the hands of everyone involved. And put their names in the area for which they are responsible.

Keep a musical bed going throughout the segue.

Rather than stop playing at the end of the song, the guitar or keys can underscore the verbal transition and prayer to the offering. The musical bed, while hardly noticed by most, will be a constant thread through the preceding song, the prayer for the offering, and into the next element.

Keep comments brief and focused on the offering

Often pastors and lay leaders will use this time to add or augment announcements. If you want to keep a worshipful flow into and out of the offering, take the advice of Red Leader: "Cut the chatter, Red Two." (Sorry, inner Star Wars geek leaking out.)

Prep your ushers

These are good guys just waiting to be told what to do, and willing to do it. Don't wait till the prayer before the offering to give them instructions. Also, create a default mode for them that will work 99% of the time. For instance, instruct them that they should be getting into place during the song (or whatever the element is) before the offering. As the pastor or leader steps up to pray, they walk forward. No verbal cues needed.

Cue up whatever is next

Whether you are watching a video, singing another worship song, or having a special number, make sure that element is ready to launch as soon as the prayer finishes. Again, keeping that musical bed going until this next element will further connect the pieces.

In the next chapter, we'll continue talking about how to make great segues in and out of the offering, and even ideas on how to do the offering in a way that creates flow.

Segue #15: The Offering

Part II

In the last section, we looked at some of the potential pitfalls that can lead up to the offering. We also looked at ways to prepare our people and flow smoothly into this portion of the service. This section is going to give some more suggestions for flowing in, out, and through the offering time. Some may work for you, others could get you fired. As with all my ideas and suggestions, take what works and ignore what doesn't.

What to Do During the Offering

I know, this series is about segues, but if we're honest, what accompanies the offering is, in a sense, a segue. The offering is the main thing. It's what we're really after. Not in a greedy way, but in a "Let's keep our lights on and feed the youth pastor's kids" way.

The offering might be the most tangible act of worship for some people: a true sacrifice unto God. But unlike other elements of corporate worship, it's highly individualized and momentary. Once a person chooses to give and prepares his offering (writing a check, putting cash in an envelope, or in many cases now, setting up online giving), the actual offering only engages that worshiper for the six seconds that he watches the plate arrive on his right, and the two seconds it takes to pass it to the left.

It might help us to look at whatever accompanies the offering as a *secondary element of worship*, and really, one big segue. It's not less important; it's just serving the main thing of the moment. It moves us from the prayer, throughout the passing, and on to the next element.

Let's get back to what to do during the offering. The usual suspect is the offertory, often referred to as *special music*. Does that cause anyone else to shudder? I have heard everyone from Bible college professors to armchair theologians rail against the notion of special music. *Are you saying our other worship music isn't special?*

That's not my issue with it. The problem with special music is that after a while, it's not that special. *Especially* if your soloist line-up isn't too deep.

To bring the *specialness* back to specials, we could try a couple things. One, we should up the ante significantly, which is hard to do week after week. Even excellence gets taken for granted over time. Two, we could limit the number of specials performed, so they are unique, high-quality moments that bless people.

So without the special, what do we use to segue through the offering?

Can we keep being real here? Few churches struggle with filling time. Most have enough content to fill two services. Is it wrong to look at our offering as a time to accomplish some other things? This time could be used to accomplish:

A Scripture Reading
Maybe one that tees up the message, or one that leads to the next set of worship songs.

Another Set of Worship Music
We do this most Sundays at my church. It's a great place to do a new or newer song. People are sitting and more relaxed. They can just take in the words. A side benefit to this approach is that it eliminates another hand-off. It allows the worship leader, or even one of the vocalists, to intro the offering and pray into it.

A Faith Story or Testimony
We will talk about transitioning into these in an upcoming chapter.

A Video Element

A well-done and well-placed 3-minute video can move and prepare a person in ways that singing and sermons cannot. Google some of these names: Shift Worship, Worship House Media, Sermon Spice, or just search "worship videos."

Begin the Sermon

Really? Why not? The pastor is probably up front already. The beginnings of most sermons are light, so the passing of the plate wouldn't detract from it, and vice-versa.

Dismiss Kids

So the ushers may have to dodge a few ankle-biters, but this is a much better spot to let the kids go than stopping the flow between songs.

Announcements

"As the plate is being passed, grab your bulletin and let's see what's happening this week at our church." For some, this could be a sacred cow being butchered. The once special moment of tithes and offerings is now being used to hawk bake sales and Beth Moore Bible studies.

Look at it this way: it's a perfect time to connect the offering to the church's vision being played out week to week. "The reason we can have this incredible outreach this next Saturday is because of your faithful giving." And the plate being passed is a visual reinforcement of that.

You'll have to figure out what's best for your church. The offering is an act of worship. But we are stewards of the time our congregation has given us on Sunday morning. Let's make the most of it.

Vision & Mission

Segue #16: Using Segues to Communicate Vision & Mission

Vision and mission are two big buzz words that keep buzzing. They sometimes take on a new form or variation like *purpose*. And they all get attached to a *statement*. At worst, a church's vision/mission/purpose statement is ripped off from another church and then slapped on a banner or bulletin cover. At their best, these statements offer clarity about the heartbeat of the church.

This chapter won't deal with the differences of mission, vision and all that. What I want to say about it is this: if you got it, flaunt it. And here's a place to flaunt it: your segues.

If you are moving towards the offering, say something like, "Here at Trendy Metaphor Community Church, we believe God has called us to [rattle off mission/vision statement, without sounding canned]. The money you give helps us to fund [name one or two specific ministries/events/initiatives, etc.]. Thanks for giving to help change lives."

Something in your mission statement likely points towards worshiping God with our whole heart and life. So tie that in to calling people to worship. At a previous church, we had a simple mission statement: *Love God, love others, live to serve.* So inviting people into our corporate worship would go something like this, "One of our primary missions is to love God. Through worshiping Him and experiencing His love, we are able to go out to love and serve others."

This isn't rocket science. But a few extra minutes of prep during your worship serving planning can make a difference. Reread the chapter on talking transitions for other ideas on how to approach a verbal segue.

Andy Stanley says it best: "Vision leaks." You need to keep repeating and reinforcing vision in multiple ways for people to remember it and engage with it. Your worship segues are a great way to do this.

The Pre-Service

I look at the pre-service time as one big segue; it's a sequence of elements used to transition people into corporate worship. The issue with most churches in American culture is this: the majority of people don't actually come into the service until right at the start time, or likely a few minutes later. We can use a few segue elements to help move those who are there into the flow of worship. Honestly, none of these techniques will change the culture of lateness in your church, or mine. But these transition elements can help. And while each can be stand-alone tools, they will likely work better when creatively combined with other elements.

100

Segue #17: The Countdown Video

This won't really help if only 15% of that week's attendees are in the worship center when the last 30 seconds tick off. Consider running a feed to a monitor in the foyer or the kids ministry drop-off area. If running video feeds isn't in the budget right now, just run a countdown off of an independent monitor in the high traffic areas outside the sanctuary.

Segue #18: Lighting

You know what will get people's attention? Flipping the foyer lights on and off like they do at the end of intermission at the theater. Okay, that's a little crass for our setting. Save the light switch flipping to cue the prayer for the potluck or to start the next congregational meeting.

But subtle lighting changes can be an effective way to move people from pre-service chit-chat to worship. Most often, house lights (the lights above the seating area of the worship center) are bright during the pre-service time and then are dimmed noticeably as the service begins. Inversely, the stage lights brighten and bring attention to the beginning of the service. Even if you don't have a fancy light board and your only lighting controls are the switches on the back wall, you've got someone in your church who would love to serve as your lighting tech.

Segue #19: Pre-Service Music

Play recorded music during the pre-service time. Make sure you create a CD mix or playlist that fits the mood you are trying to create. And don't be afraid to push up the volume. Just keep it comfortable to talk over. Most people won't even be thinking about the music, until you fade it down quickly. That will grab people's ears and help move their attention to the front.

Couple the music fade-down with a lighting change, and you've got a strong transitional element to draw people's attention. Some will still ignore it and keep talking. You'll be tempted to ask them to shut their pie-hole so the rest of the church can worship. But don't. They might be good tithers.

Segue #20: Video Element

Dropping the lights and starting a video will move people in. Most don't want to miss a good video. It could be a funny sketch from the Skit Guys, a thought provoking vignette that will tie in with the theme of the opening worship song, or a fun promotional video for a ministry or event.

Segue #21: The Pre-Service Song

I suggested at the beginning of this section that the pre-service time is one big transition time, comprised of several of small segues, that moves people into our worship gatherings.

We can try to spiritualize this time, but let's just be honest: it's like herding cats to get our people into worship. We're competing with coffee and chit-chat in the foyer, kid check-in, and the culture of the chronicle lateness.

Often our opening song feels like a sacrificial lamb: it gives its life to bring people into the worship center. And while changing the culture of lateness in our church might be achievable before Jesus returns, it's not the point of this series. We're dealing with current reality at the moment.

So rather than fight it, or get mopey about the fact that our first song is a musical martyr, let's just re-frame our thinking and call it the "herding song." As in, it herds people into the worship center. Here are a few options for the herding song.

The Pre-Service Song
Time this song so it ends right at the beginning of the ser-

vice time. Make it more of a "sit and listen" song for those already in the service. Also, give people something to look at: put the announcement graphics on the screen, or a countdown (or both, if you've got the technology). The one big issue with the pre-service song is that people are still in your parking lot at start time. Many people aren't even there yet to be "herded."

The Opening Song

Again, get over the fact that this is likely a sacrificial lamb. Don't overlook that there will be people worshiping with this song. Pour everything you've got into this one, but don't throw your high impact song here. You know, that song we don't want people to miss. Save that tune for later.

By the time you're done with this song, most everyone will be in the worship center except those with pathological tardiness, and your youth pastor.

The Hybrid

Use a pre-service song, but begin it about two minutes before the posted service start time and let it spill into your service. This means your service will actually start 2-3 minutes late (though this might actually be early for some of you).

"But," you ask, "isn't this enabling lateness?"

Yep. But remember, we're dealing with current reality. When I originally wrote this blog post, this was my church's reality. However, when we moved into our new building, we decided it was time change this. One of the tactics[6] was to stop using this "hybrid" approach that spilled into our service time. When we do a pre-service song, which is most weeks, we plan it to end right at the beginning of the service.

Before we wrap up this section, let me throw out a few options for your pre-service song:

- Use a familiar, upbeat song that the worship team can play in its sleep. That way there is not extra work for the team, plus they can relax and have fun with it. People will be drawn in by that.
- Another option is to introduce a new song. When I introduce a new song, I will run it 3-4 weeks in a row as a live pre-service song. This sounds like a lot, but at best, the average church attendee will likely hear it twice. And it gives my team the chance to play and sing it at least once, depending on the team rotation.

---

6 Another tactic to curb lateness is the closing of the main doors in the auditorium at service time. That communicates clearly that we begin on time. We have a secondary door that allows latecomers to be less distracting as they come in. One member jokingly refers to it as the "door of shame"

- Try a "pre-prise"[7]: use a song that you'll be doing later in the service, especially if it is a new one. That will help get it in people's heads. Just don't do the opening song, or it will feel really long if you play it twice back to back.

Again, each of these pre-service segues are best used in conjunction with others. Try different combinations. Remember that what works now won't work for long. People can become as conditioned to a pre-service song as they are to Muzak in a department store. Do you remember hearing music on your last trip to JCPenney?

---

7 As opposed to a "reprise".

Segue #22: The Pre-Service As A Preparation Time

I once attended a Sunday evening service at Parkside Church near Cleveland to hear Alistair Begg preach. A Scottish accent always makes a sermon better. It was a typical traditional pre-service time with soft music, dim lights and people chit-chatting with folks they hadn't seen for at least a week. Pastor Begg got up and said, "It sounds like your voices are in fine shape tonight." Folks gave the usual polite chuckle. But before the obligatory laughter died down, the Scotsman firmly shot out, "But you'd be better to prepare your hearts before the Lord." The place got real quiet, real quick.

A quiet preparation time before the service is likely a thing of the past for many churches. However, it might not hurt to implement it occasionally. I say occasionally just because anything that's done weekly runs the risk of losing its effectiveness.

If your church wants to try to create the pre-service preparation time, consider some of the elements you need to create that environment.

- A sign outside the worship center encouraging people to enter quietly.

- Doors closed to the foyer or lobby. This will create a feeling of entering in. It also cuts the noise from the gabbers in the lobby.
- Soft music. It could be canned music or live acoustic guitar/piano playing softly.
- Dim lighting. Bright overhead lighting doesn't encourage quiet and reflective moments.
- Scriptures or short devotional quotes looping on the screen.
- Candles.
- Pictures of nature.
- People in prayer or worship.
- A written guide in the bulletin or screen to help people know how to prepare for worship.

Here are a few other things that you should consider with a pre-service preparation time.

- You will always have the chit-chatters in the foyer, so you still have to figure out some way to bring them in.
- This time could be off-putting to guests, especially non-Christians. Or, it might be just what they've been looking for. You can't please everyone. Just be clear about what you want. Don't try to make it conducive for preparation *and* chit-chatting. People won't know what to do. My two cents: If you're not

going for quiet preparation, I'd always go for the other end: a bright and celebratory environment.

- Your service may need to begin differently. Jumping right in with the typical upbeat opener will be a little jarring to those who have been in there. Consider starting with a quieter slower song, and building up. Or sing the chorus of a faster song softer and at a lower tempo. Then build tempo and volume to move people into the song as usual.

As we wrap up the transitions that deal with the pre-service time, here's a last thought as you think through this stuff. *Whatever you find that works to bring your people in at the beginning will most likely not work next month or even next week.* People will start ignoring that countdown after they've seen it a few times and the live music will become background noise. That's just how it is. So it's up to us to be creative and help segue people into worship.

Segue #23: Videos

Part I

At my first full-time ministry job, I was the youth and worship guy at a two-pastor church. By default, that also meant I was the substitute sermon guy. (Have you ever noticed senior pastors aren't into *quid pro quo*? They never act as the substitute youth guy. Studies show that this is actually a relief to 4 out of 4 students.)

When my senior pastor was to be gone, I would phone in my youth lessons for a couple weeks while I prepped a message. At that time, only the young and hip pastors used movie clips. I was young and cool (or so I thought), so it was a no-brainer. And since *The Lord of the Rings* was up for canonization just behind the Narnia books, it would have pretty much been a sin not to use them. Plus, I figured I had a better chance of escaping church discipline with a title like *Return of the King* versus *Bruce Almighty*. After sermon subbing three or four times, an elderly lady approached me and said, "If you keep preaching, I'm going to end up seeing that entire film, aren't I?" Point taken. Cue *Bruce Almighty*.

Fast forward over a decade and video clips are as common

today as bad bulletin clip art was in the 90s. We have video coming out our ears. There are at least a dozen different worship video ministries in the vein of Worship House Media. Publishers and other ministries crank out promotional clips to hawk everything from Beth Moore Bible studies to building orphanages in Haiti. And don't forget the amateur Spielbergs in our own pews. You might even be one of the churches that have the sermon on video, taped at a previous service on a different campus.

Here's one thing to remember: there's nothing so high quality in your service that can't be at least partially ruined by a bad segue. Videos are no exception. If you ripped the final race scene from *Secretariat* the moment it hit Netflix, Big Red might as well have lost at Belmont if the transition in or out boogers the moment. In other words, if the video lurches in as it begins with the sound at 100 dB, it will take people several seconds to get their mind on what is being shown. The same goes for a poorly executed exit. Whatever point is being made will get bumped from their brains by a bad ending.

This segue is simple: whenever you pull clips from movies, YouTube, or create your own videos, take the extra time and edit a dissolve at both ends of the clip. Make sure you apply a fade to the audio as well. iMovie and Windows Movie Maker are about as simple as they come and can get the job done easily. Adobe Premiere Elements will run you the better part of a Benjamin, but it will give you more editing power than the average church video clip will ever need.

Does video editing freak you out? Here's the best news of the whole chapter: projection software (like MediaShout, ProPresenter, EasyWorship) can transition your clips to black or crossfade them with the graphics on either side. No editing required. This alone should make it worth upgrading to a projection software. Not to mention that PowerPoint for lyric projection went out with neckties for pastors. Just speaking the truth in love.

There's one more segue for videos that is worth talking about. And that is, talking about the videos themselves.

Segue #24: Videos

Part II

In the last chapter, we talked about how to keep the beginning and end of video clips from disrupting the flow of your service. Now we will discuss the *dos* and *don'ts* of verbally transitioning the video.

DO give enough background for people to understand the context of a movie clip.
DON'T explain everything they will see. Let the clip do the work. And don't explain the entire plot of the movie. If they like it, they'll watch it.

DO intentionally create anticipation. If you're going to talk about it, find some way to whet people's appetites for what they are about to see.
DON'T set the clip up as the funniest, coolest, most incredible clip they will ever watch. Because, it just might not be. Also, make sure you know if it really is a hip, cutting-edge video before saying so. You might just have discovered the Numa Numa kid ten years after it went viral.

DO work hard on the verbal segue into and out of your video. A little thought into our talking transitions goes a long way.

DON'T give away the *tie in* or lesson before you show the clip. People are smart. Most of the time, they will connect with the point you're trying to make before you make it. If you have to work that hard to explain the connection, is it really the right video? Or is it just something you like and want to sneak in the service?

DO consider not talking at all. A lot of videos won't need a set up. And if you plan not to talk beforehand...
DON'T forget to tell your tech that you won't be introducing the video. (This is one of those hand-offs we talked about earlier in the series.)

Before we move on to other segues, a few parting thoughts about segues to and from videos.

Lighting

If you have the capability to dim your lighting, do so. Sometimes, that's all the cue you need to get people to look up at a screen. Hopefully the same people that dimmed your lights will bring them back up for you. If you have to ask, you've got some work to do.

Sound

If your sound tech is doing the muting, make sure he or she

unmutes the audio channel for the video *before* it starts.

Simple Seating Segue

If you are finishing a song and going into a video, say something simple like, "You can be seated now as this clip begins." This does a couple things. It seats our people (people who, six days a week, know how to sit and stand without being told, but somehow we suck that decision-making process from their prefrontal cortex every Sunday). And it gives a not-so-subtle cue to your tech to start the video.

The Last Thing

People know what dead air is. We have been trained by our TVs to squirm after two seconds of undefined time. The moment we direct people to the screens and nothing happens, they begin to unconsciously disconnect from the journey we have invited them on. Of all the ways we hope to encourage people to express worship to God, squirming is not high on the list. So make sure you...

1. Determine your cue
2. Communicate the cue with your tech
3. Clearly give the cue when it's time

Connecting to the Message

Segue #25: Connecting to the Message through Prayer

For our last four segues, we'll be looking at elements we've already discussed but using them to transition to the message. First let's discuss prayer.

Prayer before the message does a few things:
1. It gives time for people to prepare, both in their hearts and head
2. It invites the Holy Spirit to work through the text and message
3. It helps the pastor center in on what he is about to do.

We've used prayer a few times to segue between various elements. And that almost sounds crass. No, it does sound crass. I'll just admit that writing through a series like this I've had to ask myself more than once, "Am I more concerned about segues or the Savior?" Am I using prayer (communication with a Holy God) just to connect to the next thing in the service?

That's something we all have to wrestle with. I go back to what I wrote in the introduction: transitions will happen whether I plan them or not. But good transitions move the congregation along from one segment to the next, hopefully without detracting from what the worshipers just experienced, or are about to experience.

With that considered, prayer (as well as reading scripture) is an act of worship, something that can stand on its own as an expression of corporate worship. But that doesn't mean it shouldn't be woven into the tapestry of the gathering in such a way that it moves our hearts and carries our attention to another moment of worship. And that's what prayer does here.

Consider a few things as you use prayer to segue to the message:

Who prays?
Is it the preaching pastor? Or worship leader? Or does an elder get up to pray? Regardless, have a plan. As the previous element is ending, the person praying needs to be getting in place before it concludes.

What is prayed?
Is this the lengthier "pastoral prayer" that some churches practice, a time to pray for missionaries and the head deaconess's sick cousin in Akron? Or is it simply an "open the eyes of our heart" kind of prayer to prepare for the mes-

sage? It's good to define this, especially if you've got some-one other than the preaching pastor praying. The pastor will start to get a little twitchy if the prayer starts rambling into the message time.

What else is going on?

- Whenever you move from a musical element, I'd say underscore that prayer with soft keys or acoustic guitar. That adds another layer of connection in the segue.
- Is prayer a time for the music team to quietly exit the stage? Some churches are into this. Some aren't. But regardless, have a plan to get the team off the stage with minimal distraction.
- If the teaching pastor isn't the one praying, he or she should be moving into place.

This transition to the message might seem like a something that can just be done on the fly. After all, it's a time that ev-eryone knows is coming. But the movement to the message is a turning point in the service. We are deliberately open-ing God's word to hear what He has to say to us. A segue of prayer is a fitting preparation for this.

Segue #26: Connecting to the Message through Video

A few segues ago, we talked about the ins and outs, literally, of using videos. In that case, the clip was the service element we were transitioning to and from. But now we're using a video to get us to the next thing: the message.

Since the decisions for this segue are up to the preaching/teaching pastors, I am going to direct my comments to them. The rest of you can listen in.

Dear Teaching Pastors,

There are a few different kinds of videos you could use to make the transition:

The Movie Clip

Hopefully you are showing this because it illustrates a main point or application of your message. Remember, only youth pastors have the luxury of showing movie clips that are completely unrelated to their talks. (But at least you get the chance to show movie clips. The only videos worship pastors get to use are swirly motion backgrounds behind the song lyrics.)

For this to be a true segue to the message, you will need to run it between your message and the preceding element. You might need to set it up, but sometimes it's better if you don't. Keep us guessing while we watch it. It's creates a little positive tension and anticipation.

The Sermon Illustration Video

You usually have two choices on these kinds of videos. The first is a light-hearted, humorous sketch that gets a point across with some laughs. The second is some sort of emotion-tugging vignette that evokes either guilt or tears (or both) and usually has a Casting Crowns song playing in the background. Go with the laughs. None of us are ready for "Every Man" right out of the chute.

The "Man on the Street" Interview

Just make sure the question being asked actually applies to your message. Even though you like watching Kirk Cameron going all "Ten Commandments" on some pagan, that really won't segue us to a message on tithing. Except if you promise to never to show Kirk Cameron videos again if we promise to put more in the offering each week. That would tie in to tithing and cheerful giving.

Testimony/Faith Story Video

This could range from some personal stories in your church,

stories from the mission fields you support, or even faith stories are resonating around the country or world. The latter you can find on SermonSpice.com and similar sites.

Scripture Video

This might be something produced by one of the worship video production companies, or you can go homemade. Record the scripture being read by a talented reader. Add some background music and text for visuals. The video part could easily be accomplished by your projection software. And if you don't have a reader, use a clip from an audio Bible, just don't use that version that sounds like Vincent Price read it. There are several audio Bibles out there now that have been read by celebrities. So you could actually have Samuel L. Jackson, Brad Paisley's wife, or Bo Duke reading your passage for next Sunday.

As with any videos, apply the same good practice of fading in and out, and setting up the clip (if needed).

Segue #27: Connecting to the Message through Readings

One simple way to segue to the sermon is by using scripture text that the pastor's message is based on. I touched on this segue in the last chapter by suggesting the use of video to present the scripture. That's one option. Another option is a "worship team reader." Don't discount the power of gifted readers. They often will do a better job than the pastor at reading the selected text for that morning. Just like having a team of talented vocalists who sing, build a team of talented readers who, well, read.

Here's what to look for:

A good sounding voice.
They don't need to sound like the movie trailer announcers (unless you're reading from the book of Revelation). But they do need to have pleasant sounding voices.

Expressiveness in reading.
Look for people with acting experience. Or people who enjoy getting up at poetry readings. Just make sure they are not over-the-top and dripping with too much expressiveness.

A love for scripture and a respect for this position.
This person might have the ability to read it well even if they see it for the first time that morning. But your congregation will sense it if the reader has been soaking up that scripture during the week.

Here are some ways to facilitate this:

- *Communicate the passage as early in the week as possible.*
  Be clear on which translation you want. And a note to pastors: consider using a different translation than what you are preaching from, especially if the passage is familiar. A paraphrased Bible like the Message can shake people from autopilot listening. But if the Message sounds too wonky (because let's admit it, while we love Eugene Peterson, the Message does sound a little wonky in places), try something like the New Living Translation or Contemporary English Version.
- *Be clear on when the reader is to begin.*
  And give instructions on moving into place before the previous element finishes. The ending of a song can provide a good starting point, and the piano or guitar can just continue playing to underscore the reading. Coming out of this reading, the pastor can simply start his message or pray.

- *Be clear on where the reader should stand.*
  And which mic to use. And does he need a music stand? Does the sound tech know this is happening?
- *Reinforce the scripture with visuals.*
  Many people love having the scripture read to them. They probably are audible learners. Me, I'm checked out within two sentences, unless the reader is especially engaging. I'm a visual learner. And there are a lot of people like me, so put the text on the screen. You can also invite people to follow along from their Bible, unless it's a not-so-common translation for your church. Then people think more about the difference between the two versions than what's being said. By the way, kinesthetic learners, I'm not sure what to tell you in order to pay attention. Maybe you need to be the upfront reader and do interpretive movements while you read. Just a suggestion.

For more ideas for scripture reading, see Segue #12 part 1 and part 2.

Segue #28: The Introduction

For the last few chapters of the segue series, we have focused on segues to the sermon. I've suggested video, music, scripture, prayer, pyrotechnics and origami demonstrations. Okay, so we didn't use the last two, but those would be really cool. Unless you did them on the same Sunday. Then it's just a fire hazard.

For the final segue to the message (and overall final segue, unless I go past this randomly chosen number of 28), we're going to talk about the Introduction.

This is the oldest segue known to man. When the population of the earth doubled during a nap, it was an introduction that segued history:

God: *Adam, while you were asleep, I made you something.*

Adam: *Awesome, God, what is it? And why does my side feel funky?*

God: *Oh, um, I think you slept on it wrong. Never mind that. I'd like you to meet Eve.*

Adam: *Whoa, dude!*

God: *Actually, wo-man. Now go try out the "Be Fruitful and Multiply" app I installed in you two. It's better than Mine-craft.*

And thus began the first (and only) relationship on earth that did not involve head games. At least for a while.

Here are some reasons to use an introduction:

Guest Guessing Game

If you're visiting a church and some guy just gets up and starts preaching, you kind of assume he's the pastor. But it's still nice to know.

Pavlov's Pastor

In most of our churches, we've conditioned our folks to expect a certain who, what, and when. When the "what" comes (the message) and it's the wrong "who" (the youth pastor), there's an oh-so-slight disconcerting moment. (Unless you think the youth pastor's an idiot – then you're just plain tweaked.) The introduction really is a favor to both the guest speaker and the congregation.

Bad Wrap

It's a great way to transition out of another "talking" element, like the announcements. When someone besides the senior pastor does announcements, that person often doesn't know how to wrap.

"So yeah, there are the announcements. I think that's all we have. Anything else? No? Um, Okay then. Well, thanks for listening. I'm going to go sit over there by my wife now...."

A simple fix is to give the announcement guy something concrete to end his time. "While Pastor Smith is coming up, open your Bibles to Matthew 18 as we continue our series on forgiving people you think are idiots."

The above illustrates a call-to-action ("open your Bibles") with a quick summary of the topic or series. This can work well as an introduction. It gives the pastor and the congregation a moment to settle in to the beginning of the message.

What doesn't always work so well is the Tonight Show-*esque* "and now let's welcome our pastor!!!" *If no* one claps, it's a little awkward. And most pastors I know would *not* want to be introduced like that. If he does, bad segues are the least of that church's problems.

Conclusion

I hope this resource has giving you plenty of tips, tricks and tactics to make great transitions worship elements. But I also hope it's inspired you to come up with your own ideas.

The key is planning and preparation. If your church has never really bothered to create intentional flow in worship, you may face some resistance. My team used to balk at the idea of practicing the segues between songs, but now it's just a part of our rehearsal. I also used to create worship service scripts that no one read. Now we have an all-hands meeting every Sunday with everyone involved in the service to talk through all the elements, especially transitions. Why? Because we know if something will go wrong, it's likely going to happen in the hand-offs.

So if you're just starting out, start simple. The flow you achieve in worship will be noticed and appreciated (by most), and it will give you the credibility to begin to build better segues into every part of your service.

Bonus Section

These bonuses can be found at
worshipteamcoach.com/WFBonus

Scripture Montage

We discussed scripture montages back in Segue #12 on page 63. The following are montages that I've used in worship.

The Stand

Our Standing

Who may ascend the hill of the Lord?
Who may stand in his holy place?
He who has clean hands and a pure heart,
who does not lift up his soul to an idol
or swear by what is false.

(Psalm 24:3-4)

So, if you think you are standing firm, be careful that you don't fall! No temptation has seized you except what is common to man. And God is faithful; he will not let you be tempted beyond what you can bear. But when you are tempted, he will also provide a way out so that you can stand up under it.

(1 Corinthians 10:12-13)

If you, O Lord, kept a record of sins,
O Lord, who could stand?

But with you there is forgiveness;
therefore you are feared.

(Psalm 130:3-4)

Therefore, since we have been justified through faith,
we have peace with God through our Lord Jesus Christ,
through whom we have gained access by faith into this
grace in which we now stand.

(Romans 5:1-2a)

Therefore, my dear brothers, stand firm. Let nothing
move you. Always give yourselves fully to the work of
the Lord, because you know that your labor in the Lord
is not in vain.

(1 Corinthians 15:58)

Now it is God who makes both us and you stand firm in
Christ. He anointed us, set his seal of ownership on us,
and put his Spirit in our hearts as a deposit, guarantee-
ing what is to come.

(2 Corinthians 1:21-22)

Christ Stands

I know that my Redeemer lives,
and that in the end he will stand upon the earth.

(Job 19:25)

In that day the Root of Jesse will stand as a banner for the peoples; the nations will rally to him, and his place of rest will be glorious.

(Isaiah 11:10)

Here I am! I stand at the door and knock. If anyone hears my voice and opens the door, I will come in and eat with him, and he with me.

(Revelation 3:20)

Then I saw a Lamb, looking as if it had been slain, standing in the center of the throne, encircled by the four living creatures and the elders.

(Revelation 5:6)

Our response

Written as corporate prayer

Lord, we have heard of your fame;

we stand in awe of your deeds, O Lord.

Renew them in our day,

in our time make them known…

(Habakkuk 3:2)

Rock Reading

In Psalm 40, David says this:

I waited patiently for the Lord;

he turned to me and heard my cry.

He lifted me out of the slimy pit,

out of the mud and mire;

He set my feet on a rock

and gave me a firm place to stand.

(Psalm 40:1-2)

1000 years later, Peter tells us exactly who this Rock is:
As you come to him, the living Stone—rejected by humans but chosen by God and precious to him— you also, like living stones, are being built into a spiritual house to be a holy priesthood, offering spiritual sacrifices acceptable to God through Jesus Christ. For in Scripture it says:
"See, I lay a stone in Zion,

a chosen and precious cornerstone,

and the one who trusts in him

will never be put to shame."

(Psalm 40:4-6)

Great I Am

Jesus declares this about himself in the book of Revelation:

"I am the Alpha and the Omega," says the Lord God, "who is, and who was, and who is to come, the Almighty."

I am the First and the Last. I am the Living One; I was dead, and behold I am alive for ever and ever! And I hold the keys of death and Hades.

(Revelation 1:8; 17b, 18)

In response to greatness of the I Am, all of heaven worships him with these words:

"Holy, holy, holy
is the Lord God Almighty,
who was, and is, and is to come."

(Rev 4:8)

Let's worship the Great I Am...
(begin with chorus – slower, quiet, then into verse)

Resurrection

On his arrival, Jesus found that Lazarus had already been in the tomb for four days. Bethany was less than two miles from Jerusalem, and many Jews had come to Martha and Mary to comfort them in the loss of their brother. When Martha heard that Jesus was coming, she went out to meet him, but Mary stayed at home.

"Lord," Martha said to Jesus, "if you had been here, my brother would not have died. But I know that even now God will give you whatever you ask."

Jesus said to her, "Your brother will rise again."

Martha answered, "I know he will rise again in the resurrection at the last day."

Jesus said to her, "I am the resurrection and the life. He who believes in me will live, even though he dies; and whoever lives and believes in me will never die. Do you believe this?"

"Yes, Lord," she told him, "I believe that you are the Christ, the Son of God, who was to come into the world."
(John 11:17-27)
I want to know Christ and the power of his resurrection

and the fellowship of sharing in his sufferings, becoming like him in his death, 11 and so, somehow, to attain to the resurrection from the dead.

(Philippians 3:10-11)

The Spirit of God, who raised Jesus from the dead, lives in you. And just as God raised Christ Jesus from the dead, he will give life to your mortal bodies by this same Spirit living within you.

(Romans 8:11)

Praise be to the God and Father of our Lord Jesus Christ! In his great mercy he has given us new birth into a living hope through the resurrection of Jesus Christ from the dead, 4 and into an inheritance that can never perish, spoil or fade —kept in heaven for you

(1 Peter 1:3-4)

But let me reveal to you a wonderful secret. We will not all die, but we will all be transformed! It will happen in a moment, in the blink of an eye, when the last trumpet is blown. For when the trumpet sounds, those who have died will be raised to live forever. And we who are living will also be transformed. For our dying bodies must be transformed into bodies that will never die; our mortal bodies must be transformed into immortal bodies.

Then, when our dying bodies have been transformed into bodies that will never die, this Scripture will be fulfilled:

"Death is swallowed up in victory.

O death, where is your victory?

O death, where is your sting?"

For sin is the sting that results in death, and the law gives sin its power. But thank God! He gives us victory over sin and death through our Lord Jesus Christ.

(1 Corinthians 15:51-57)

Name Scriptures, Shorter

I will praise you forever for what you have done;
in your name I will hope, for your name is good.
I will praise you in the presence of your saints.

(Psalm 52:9)

Yes, LORD, walking in the way of your laws, we wait for
you; your name and renown are the desire of our hearts.

(Isaiah 26:8)

May his name endure forever; may it continue as long as
the sun.
All nations will be blessed through him, and they will
call him blessed.

(Psalm 72:17)

Who will not fear you, O Lord,
and bring glory to your name?
For you alone are holy.
All nations will come
and worship before you,
for your righteous acts have been revealed."

(Revelation 15:4)

He provided redemption for his people;
he ordained his covenant forever—

holy and awesome is his name.

(Psalm 111:9)

Salvation is found in no one else, for there is no other name under heaven given to men by which we must be saved."

(Acts 4:12)

Therefore God exalted him to the highest place
and gave him the name that is above every name,
that at the name of Jesus every knee should bow,
in heaven and on earth and under the earth,
and every tongue confess that Jesus Christ is Lord,
to the glory of God the Father.

(Philippians 2:9)

Name Scriptures

O LORD, our Lord,
how majestic is your name in all the earth!
You have set your glory above the heavens.

(Psalm 8:1)

Ascribe to the LORD the glory due his name; worship
the LORD in the splendor of his holiness.

(Psalm 29:2)

I will praise you forever for what you have done;
in your name I will hope, for your name is good.
I will praise you in the presence of your saints.

(Psalm 52:9)

Yes, LORD, walking in the way of your laws, we wait for
you; your name and renown are the desire of our hearts.

(Isaiah 26:8)

May his name endure forever;
may it continue as long as the sun.
All nations will be blessed through him,
and they will call him blessed.

(Psalm 72:17)

Who will not fear you, O Lord,

and bring glory to your name?
For you alone are holy.
All nations will come
and worship before you,
for your righteous acts have been revealed."
(Revelation 15:4)

In his name the nations will put their hope."
(Matthew 12:21)

He provided redemption for his people;
he ordained his covenant forever—
holy and awesome is his name.
(Psalm 111:9)

Yet to all who received him, to those who believed in his
name, he gave the right to become children of God.
(John 1:12)

And everyone who calls on the name of the Lord will be
saved.'
(Acts 2:21)

Salvation is found in no one else, for there is no other name under heaven given to men by which we must be saved."

(Acts 4:12)

Therefore God exalted him to the highest place
and gave him the name that is above every name,
that at the name of Jesus every knee should bow,
in heaven and on earth and under the earth,
and every tongue confess that Jesus Christ is Lord,
to the glory of God the Father.

(Philippians 2:9)

Power in the Name of Jesus

For the message of the cross is foolishness to those who are perishing, but to us who are being saved it is the power of God.

(1 Corinthians 1:18)

I want to know Christ and the power of his resurrection and the fellowship of sharing in his sufferings, becoming like him in his death, 11and so, somehow, to attain to the resurrection from the dead.

(Philippians 3:10-11)

For in Christ all the fullness of the Deity lives in bodily form, and you have been given fullness in Christ, who is the head over every power and authority.

(Colossians 2:9-10)

Therefore God exalted him to the highest place
and gave him the name that is above every name,
that at the name of Jesus every knee should bow,
in heaven and on earth and under the earth,
and every tongue confess that Jesus Christ is Lord,
to the glory of God the Father.

(Philippians 2:9-11)

Like You

Then my soul will rejoice in the Lord
and delight in his salvation.
My whole being will exclaim,
"Who is like you, O Lord ?
You rescue the poor from those too strong for them,
the poor and needy from those who rob them."
(Psalm 35:9-10)

Your righteousness reaches to the skies, O God,
you who have done great things.
Who, O God, is like you?
(Psalm 71:19)

Among the gods there is none like you, O Lord;
no deeds can compare with yours.
(Psalm 86:8)

O Lord God Almighty, who is like you?
You are mighty, O LORD, and your faithfulness sur-
rounds you.
(Psalm 89:8)

God's Greatness

Your ways, O God, are holy.
What god is so great as our God?
(Psalm 77:13)

How great are your works, O LORD,
how profound your thoughts!
(Psalm 92:5)

All the nations you have made
will come and worship before you, O Lord;
they will bring glory to your name.
For you are great and do marvelous deeds;
you alone are God.
(Psalm 86:9-10)

"Great and marvelous are your deeds,
Lord God Almighty.
Just and true are your ways, King of the ages.
Who will not fear you, O Lord,
and bring glory to your name?
For you alone are holy.
All nations will come
and worship before you,
for your righteous acts have been revealed."
(Revelation 15:3b-4)

Great is the LORD and most worthy of praise;
his greatness no one can fathom.

(Psalm 145:3)

Segue Bonus Worksheets

These charts are available for download at worshipteamcoach.com/WFBonus.

Segue Worksheet: Sunday, August 23

Service Element	Segue	Additional Notes
Pre service song – Your Grace Finds Me		
	As song ends, WL welcomes congregation. Drummer starts click. Keys fade in. After welcome, drummer counts in.	House lights dim as Opening Song Starts
Opening Song: Open Up the Heavens		
	At end reprise bridge, stop click. WL prays. Pastor Bob comes up during prayer and seats people when WL is done.	Tell Pastor Bob about bridge reprise so he doesn't come up early.
Welcome/Announcements		
	Pastor Bob invites congregation to stand and enter back into worship through music. Drummer counts in as people are standing	Keep G Pad loop running through both of these songs...
This is Amazing Grace		
	End with outro. Clap offering. During clap offering, drummer starts click and keyboard player starts intro.	Encourage vocalists to be lead out clapping during applause for the Lord.
As We Pray		
	End with outro. Clap offering. During clap offering acoustic guitar begins noodling in key of G.	
Scripture reading – Psalm 103 Underscored by acoustic guitar		
	As scripture finishes, guitar begins playing intro to How Marvelous	
How Marvelous		
	As song ends, pray. During prayer ushers get into place	Video tech – have clip ready to go. Audio – have video channel unmuted.
Offering / Missions Video		
	As last 10 seconds of video finishes, Pastor Bob comes up to platform	Send Bob link to video so he knows the end.
Message		
	Pastor Bob invites the worship team up, and prays to close his message. WL invites people to stand during intro	Keys underscore his prayer. Make sure keyboardist knows to get up quick and start noodling in the key of A.
The Stand		
	As song ends, WL gives planned benediction and dismisses people. Tech fades up music as he finishes.	
Post – service recorded music		Let's go eat some Chipotle...

© 2014 WorshipTeamCoach.com & Jon Nicol | Part of WorshipFlow: 28 Ways to Create Great Segues
Permission is given to copy and distribute this worksheet.

165

Segue Worksheet:_____

Service Element	Segue	Additional Notes

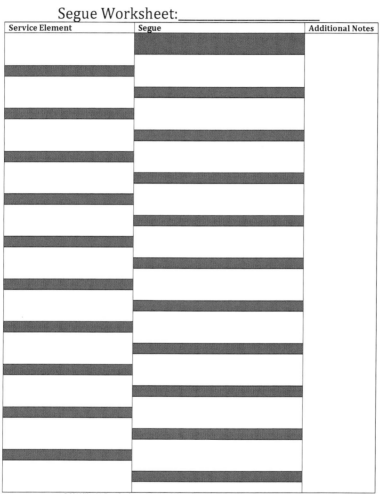

Modulation Example

In Segue #7 (page 37) we discussed using a "flat 7" chord to modulate to a new key. We use this technique between verses 2 and 3 in our arrangement of Holy, Holy, Holy.

This chart is available for download at worshipteamcoach. com/WFBonus.

Holy, Holy, Holy

Heber/Dykes

About the Author

Jon Nicol is a worship pastor, teacher and blogger from Lexington, OH. He and his wife planned to have three children and ended up with four incredible kids. He's the worship pastor at Heartland Church in Lexington and founded WorshipTeam-Coach.com to coach and train worship leaders and teams. You can find more worship resources there, including his blog.

Follow Jon on Twitter: **@jonnicol**

Contact him through email: **jon@worshipteamcoach.com**

Made in the
USA
Middletown, DE